fashion
sourcebooks

The 1950s

John Peacock

Fashion Sourcebooks The 1950s

With 310 illustrations

Thames and Hudson

For Marion James

© 1997 Thames and Hudson Ltd,
London

All rights reserved. No part
of this publication may be
reproduced or transmitted
in any form or by any means,
electronic or mechanical, including
photocopy, recording or any other
information storage and retrieval
system, without prior permission
in writing from the publisher.

British Library Cataloguing-
in-Publication Data
A catalogue record for this book is
available from the British Library

ISBN 0-500-27931-4

Printed and bound in Slovenia
by Mladinska Knjiga

Contents

On 12 February 1947 Christian Dior launched his 'Corolle' line, the first collection from his recently opened fashion house. Instantly nicknamed the 'New Look', it brought a luxury, femininity and grace to postwar fashion, and had a dramatic, transforming effect on the female silhouette. The 'New Look' would almost completely dominate the greater part of the next decade.

This Sourcebook for the 1950s shows the development of women's fashion from the comparatively early days of the 'New Look', when the square shoulders and masculine details of the 1940s still lingered, through the ultra-feminine and luxurious styles of the mid-1950s – clothes with gently softened shoulderlines, tiny corseted waists, roundly padded hips and long, swirling skirts only eleven inches above the ground – up to the straight, semi-fitted, knee-length 'sack' dress of the decade's end, which heralded Mary Quant's 'shifts' of the 1960s.

The glamour of films and film stars also had a profound effect on the 1950s woman, who wanted her every outfit to be suffused with elegance, sophistication and sex appeal. Figure-hugging sweaters, as worn by Marilyn Monroe and Jane Russell; Brigitte Bardot's black and white cotton gingham wedding dress, and the gamine look of Audrey Hepburn were all deeply influential.

During this period many new and easy-care fabrics were introduced, including Terylene, a man-made material which was crease-resistant but which could be permanently pleated; Orlon, a wool-like fabric, usually machine knitted; crease-resistant Banlon and Acrilan; and Poplin, a strong, hardwearing mix of man-made fibres and cotton. All these fabrics encouraged new fashions: the slender 'pencil' skirt, which lasted throughout the period, varying only in length and trim; the 'wash-and-wear' sweater; the permanently pleated skirt and the 'drip-dry' shirt.

During the Second World War men's fashion had been relatively stationary and somewhat dull, dominated as it was by military uniform. Before the 1950s it had fallen into three main categories: elegant bespoke tailoring, cheap imitations of the latter and work clothes. The introduction of ready-to-wear, the development of mass-production techniques and the new man-made fabrics gave it new life, bringing to the man-in-the-street smart suits and sports jackets, and stylish trousers with permanent creases. Nevertheless, the development of men's fashion in this period remained slow and in consequence it requires fewer illustrations than women's – the differences which do occur in the basic trends have been shown, on average, with one example for each page.

In the main, the fashions I have used are such as would have been worn by men and women of the middle or upper-middle classes and by people who, while not necessarily being 'dedicated followers of fashion', would have had a keen interest in the latest styles. The sources from which I have drawn – chiefly from Great Britain, North America, Italy and France – include contemporary magazines, catalogues and journals; museum collections; original dated photographs, and my own costume collection.

This Sourcebook is divided into ten sections, each of which includes four subdivisions covering Day Wear, Evening Wear (alternately on two occasions, Wedding Wear), Sports and Leisure Wear and a section on either Underwear or Accessories. Following the main illustrations are ten pages of schematic drawings accompanied by detailed notes about each example, giving particulars of colour, fabric, cut and trimming, as well as accessories and other useful information.

Then follow two pages of drawings which illustrate the decade 'at a glance' and which demonstrate the evolution of the period and its main development trends.

Biographies of the most important international fashion designers of the decade are also included as well as a list of further reading suggestions into the styles of this period.

1953 Evening Wear

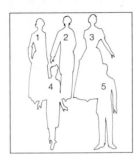

1950 Day Wear

1 Two-piece brown wool-crêpe suit: single-breasted hip-length jacket with shaped hemline, pink cotton collar which matches half-cuffs of long raglan sleeves and covered buttons, self-fabric belt with metal buckle, bloused bodice, diagonal seams which follow line of raglan sleeves and piped pockets; straight mid-calf-length skirt. Brown felt hat, curled half-brim at front, pink ribbon trim. Pink leather gloves. Flesh-coloured nylon stockings. Brown leather shoes, round toes, high thick heels. 2 Single-breasted blue wool jacket, three-button fastening, patch pockets with welt and central pleat, inset sleeves, button trim. Straight-cut grey flannel trousers, turn-ups. White collar-attached shirt. Blue wool tie. Black leather lace-up shoes, no toecaps. 3 Green and cream checked wool dress, bias-cut collar with fringed edge which matches cuffs of three-quarter-length dolman sleeves, fitted bodice with concealed front opening, green leather belt with metal buckle, flared skirt, centre-front inverted box pleat, two bias-cut shaped box pleats with button trim. Cream straw hat, wide brim. Cream leather gloves. Nylon stockings. Brown leather shoes. 4 Pale blue linen dress, bloused bodice, self-fabric buttons from under asymmetric white linen collar to waistline, self-fabric bow trim, navy-blue leather belt, metal buckle, flared skirt, unpressed box pleat, diagonal welt pockets. Pale grey brimless felt hat. Nylon stockings. Navy-blue leather shoes, peep toes, high heels. 5 Mid-calf-length beige wool coat, concealed opening, full inset sleeves tapered into button cuffs which match wrapover collar and diagonal hip-level pockets, wide self-fabric belt and buckle, flared skirt with side pleats. Small brimless brown felt hat, feather trim. Nylon stockings. Brown leather shoes, cut-away sides, round toes, high heels.

Evening Wear

1 Formal evening gown, fitted maroon silk-velvet bodice, low V-shaped neckline trimmed at point with black silk and velvet cabbage roses, drop shoulderline, wide cap sleeves, V-shaped pointed waist seam, ground-length cream corded-silk flared skirt with centre-front unpressed inverted box pleat. Above-elbow-length black silk gloves. Black jet drop earrings. Black satin strap sandals. 2 Knee-length wrapover collarless fur coat, curved front edges, hem dips to back, wide inset sleeves narrowing to wrists. Straight ankle-length black satin skirt. Black and silver drop earrings and matching necklace. Black satin shoes. 3 White tulle evening dress patterned with black flock spots, strapless fitted bodice draped over bustline, draped stole collar, full-length gathered skirt over white silk-taffeta under-skirt. Clip-on earrings and matching necklace. 4 Mid-calf-length cream satin cocktail dress embroidered with multicoloured sprays of flowers, strapless boned bodice draped over to single decorative shoulder strap, fitted straight skirt with asymmetric drapery to side hip. Drop earrings. Bead necklace. Black satin shoes, peep toes, shaped front and open sides trimmed with gold kid, ankle straps, high heels. 5 Two-piece black wool evening suit: double-breasted jacket, wide satin-faced shawl collar which matches covered button fastening and trim on cuffless inset sleeves, padded shoulders, hip-level welt pockets, breast pocket; straight-cut trousers, no turn-ups, satin stripe on outside seam. White cotton collar-attached shirt. Black satin bow-tie. Black patent-leather lace-up shoes, round toes, no toecaps.

Sports and Leisure Wear

1 Holiday wear. Pink cotton beach-dress, fitted bodice, button opening from low neckline to waistline, narrow shoulder straps, decorative triangular flaps over bustline which match triangular hip-level flap pockets and wide buckled belt, mid-calf-length panelled skirt. Green leather strap mules with flat heels. 2 Holiday wear. Pale green cotton bikini bra-top, knotted at centre front, narrow self-fabric rouleau halter straps, back fastening. Pale green linen tailored shorts, wide waistband, turn-ups, green and white striped canvas belt with metal buckle. Pink leather pumps, bow trim, flat heels. 3 Golf. Hip-length olive-green wool top, self-fabric button fastening from under small collar to point of V-shaped inset top-stitched yoke, drop shoulderline, inset shirt-style sleeves gathered into buttoned cuffs. Wide leather belt with metal buckle. Mid-calf-length olive-green, rust and cream checked wool box-pleat skirt. Olive-green brimless beret. Lace-up leather brogues, flat heels. 4 Ski wear. Two-piece weatherproof maroon cotton ski-suit: hooded hip-length top, centre-front zip fastening in bloused bodice, wide leather belt with round metal buckle, flared skirts with diagonal piped pockets; straight-cut trousers gathered on ankles, low piped pockets. Leather gauntlet mittens. Goggles. Lace-up leather ski-boots, extra strap-and-buckle fastening. 5 Walking. Hand-knitted cream wool sweater, high V-shaped neckline with ribbed edge which matches hem and cuffs of inset sleeves. Grey collar-attached wool shirt. Red and yellow spotted scarf. Narrow heavy wool knee breeches, fly fastening, strap-and-buckle fastening on knee. Knee-length hand-knitted cream wool socks. Brown leather lace-up brogues.

Underwear and Negligee

1 Sleeveless white machine-knitted cotton singlet, machine-stitched detail around low scooped neckline and armholes. White machine-knitted cotton drawers, elasticated waistband, fly front, machined hems. Red leather slippers, round toes, flat heels. 2 Cotton and lace brassiere, wired cups, light boning, elasticated panels and hem, back fastening, adjustable shoulder straps. Elasticated cotton girdle, high fitted waist, stitched front panel, embroidered motif, light boning, side zip fastening, four adjustable suspenders. Flesh-coloured nylon stockings. Pink velvet mules, white feather trim, round toes, low heels. 3 Hip-length strapless combination brassiere and girdle, wired cups trimmed with lace, light boning, elasticated front panel, stitched side panels, elasticated gussets, light boning, side zip fastening, four adjustable/removable suspenders. Flesh-coloured nylon stockings. Black ballet pumps. 4 Mid-calf-length pink nylon petticoat, fitted bodice, bra cups trimmed with lace to match gathered frill on hem of panelled skirt, self-fabric rouleau shoulder straps, side zip fastening. Pink satin ballet pumps, ribbon trim, round toes, flat heels. 5 Collarless wrapover cream nylon dressing gown, bodice gathered from shoulder yoke to waistline, full-length gathered skirts, wide self-fabric belt tied into large bow on one side, gathered elbow-length cream nylon lace sleeves. Cream satin slippers.

1951 Day Wear

1 Hip-length green and grey vertically striped flannel jacket, black astrakhan collar, two breast-level shaped flap pockets horizontally striped to match hip-level patch-and-flap pockets, connecting box pleats and shaped cuffs of long inset sleeves. Straight grey flannel skirt. Dark green felt hat, upswept brim, self-fabric bow trim. Black leather handbag and gloves. Dark green rolled umbrella, bamboo handle. Black leather shoes, mock lace-up front, high heels.
2 Blue and grey checked cloth two-piece suit: hip-length single-breasted top, shaped bias-cut pleated front panel, button fastening to under white piqué collar, grey ribbon bow tie, inset shirt sleeves, bias-cut buttoned cuffs matching waist-belt; straight skirt. Black leather shoes, bar straps. 3 Beige linen dress, buttoned strap fastening from under wing collar to knee-level ending in knife pleat, bloused bodice, narrow rouleau belt, inset sleeves, buttoned cuffs, straight skirt, double top-stitched yoke, piped pockets. Brown leather sling-back shoes, high heels.
4 Knee-length single-breasted khaki cotton weatherproof raincoat, wide lapels, raglan sleeves, diagonal hip-level welt pockets, self-fabric belt, leather buckle, horn buttons, top-stitched edges and detail. Straight-cut trousers, turn-ups. Striped collar-attached shirt. Checked tie. Brown felt trilby. Leather gloves. Brown leather lace-up shoes. 5 Fitted mid-calf-length yellow, blue and grey checked cloth coat, drop shoulderline and panel seams join to form hip-level buttoned flap pockets, piped pockets in bias-cut side panels, button fastening from waist to under collar, tight sleeves, flared skirts. Grey felt hat, feather trim. Leather gloves and handbag. Long umbrella. Navy suede shoes, scalloped edges, perforated decoration.

Evening Wear

1 Navy-blue crêpe evening dress, asymmetric draped overbodice, fitted boned strapless underbodice embroidered all over with stylized flower motifs in multicoloured glass beads, overdress with self-fabric belt, metal buckle, full-length straight skirt gathered at waist, unpressed knife pleat at front and back on one side. Long navy-blue satin gloves. Glass bead necklace matching clip-on earrings. Navy-blue satin strap sandals. 2 Pale salmon-pink organdie ball gown, fitted boned bodice, beaded and embroidered motif on centre front which matches wide shoulder straps and asymmetric overskirt, full-length gathered striped organdie underskirt worn over layers of fine tulle. 3 Oyster satin cocktail dress, fitted boned strapless bodice, mid-calf-length gored skirt, self-fabric belt with self-fabric oval buckle. Black velvet short spencer jacket, low scooped neckline with shawl collar forming bow tie fastening, elbow-length inset sleeves with cuffs. Double row of pearls matching cluster clip-on earrings. Black satin shoes. 4 White crêpe evening dress embroidered all over with yellow and black flower motifs, draped fitted boned bodice, wide shoulder straps form short draped sleeves, full-length straight skirt gathered at waist, two floating side panels gathered at waist lined with yellow silk. Elbow-length white silk gloves. Drop earrings and matching necklace. Satin shoes. 5 Black lace and silk-taffeta evening dress, fitted boned strapless bodice edged with scallops of lace which match hem above wide gathered double frills of taffeta, dips from mid-calf-length at front to ground at back. Full-length purple satin gloves. Matching set of jewelry: clip-on earrings, necklace, bracelet. Black satin shoes, peep toes, high heels.

Sports and Leisure Wear

1 Golf. Waist-length beige wool jacket, front zip fastening from base of wide waistband to under shirt-style collar, breast-level shaped patch pockets with flaps, single flap pocket with tail trim on one side of waistband, inset sleeves gathered into buttoned cuffs, top-stitched edges and detail. Mid-calf-length beige, yellow and brown checked wool box-pleated skirt. Beige felt beret with stalk. Beige wool stockings. Brown lace-up leather shoes.
2 Holiday wear. Blue and yellow striped cotton beach dress, fitted bodice with seamed bra top, V-shaped waist seam, halter straps tied at back, thigh-length skirt with wide box pleat. Natural straw hat, small crown, outsized brim, ribbon and pom-pon trim. Large beach bag which matches dress. Blue canvas sling-back shoes trimmed in white, low wedge heels. 3 Country wear. Brown and green checked wool shirt, bias-cut peter-pan collar which matches breast-level pleated patch-and-flap pockets, shoulder yoke, buttoned cuffs of inset sleeves and fringed necktie. Light brown wool straight-cut trousers with turn-ups, diagonal hip-level pockets, side fastening. Wide leather belt with metal buckle. Brown knitted wool hat, wide turned back rib with matching pom-pon. Lace-up leather shoes. 4 Tennis. Waist-length hand-knitted white cotton top, shirt-style collar trimmed with ribbing to match strap opening, edge of short sleeves and hemline. Tailored white canvas shorts with turn-ups. Lace-up white canvas sports shoes.
5 Cricket. Hand-knitted white cotton sweater, V-shaped neckline trimmed with green to match stripe above cuffs of inset sleeves and stripe above hemline. White cotton collar-attached shirt, worn open. White flannel trousers with turn-ups. White leather and canvas lace-up shoes.

Accessories

1 Cream straw hat, small crown, wide brim, raffia trim. Clip-on earrings. 2 Brimless spotted silk hat which matches outsized bow-tie. 3 Brimless hat trimmed with mimosa. 4 Pale blue straw hat, small crown, wide brim trimmed with bias-cut frill of white silk-organdie. 5 Brimless beige felt beret with stalk. 6 Yellow straw hat, turned-up brim, trimmed with posy of white flowers at back. 7 Close-fitting mesh veil, trimmed loops of silk ribbon at back. Matching set of jewelry: clip-on earrings, necklace, dress clip. Black astrakhan shoulder wrap threaded through self-fabric belt, long ends. Elbow-length black suede gloves. 8 Felt hat, small brown crown, white petersham band, cream brim. 9 Yellow straw hat, small crown, white petersham band, flared brim. 10 Black bowler hat, curled brim. Striped collar-attached hat. Spotted silk tie. 11 Dark blue trilby, narrow band. 12 Brown trilby, wide band. Yellow and brown checked silk scarf. 13 Tan and cream leather lace-up shoes. 14 Beige lace-up suede boots, rubber soles. 15 Tan leather step-in shoes. 16 Cream and tan leather shoes, perforated decoration, bow trim, high heels. 17 Navy-blue leather handbag, flap-and-stud fastening, small handle. 18 Brown leather handbag, metal stud fastening, top-stitched detail. 19 Red leather step-in shoes, bow trim, flat heels. 20 Brown leather shoes, side keyhole, white bow and trim, high heels. 21 Black leather shoes, perforated decoration, high heels. 22 Black suede shoes, peep toes, strap fronts, open sides, high heels. 23 Green leather sandals, sling-backs, ankle straps, peep toes, low heels. 24 Brown leather and snakeskin sling-back shoes, medium heels. 25 Navy-blue suede shoes, laced keyhole opening, bands of perforated decoration, medium navy-blue leather heels.

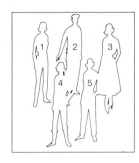

1952 Day Wear

1 Single-breasted grey wool overcoat, narrow lapels, pointed collar, raglan sleeves, buttoned strap at wrist, hip-level diagonal welt pockets, self-fabric belt, leather-covered buckle, horn buttons, top-stitched edges and detail. Straight-cut dark grey flannel trousers, turn-ups. Blue and white striped cotton collar-attached shirt. Striped silk tie. Grey trilby, narrow band, curled brim. Leather gloves. Black leather lace-up shoes, no toe-caps. **2** Mid-calf-length light blue wool coat, concealed opening, hip-level vertical welt pockets, raglan sleeves gathered into deep cuffs, large grey fox-fur collar. Brimless grey felt hat cut away on one side. Grey leather gloves. Nylon stockings. Grey suede shoes, round toes, high heels. **3** Cream cotton dress patterned with red, wide top-stitched tuck at bust-level to give effect of overbodice which matches double yoke above mid-calf-length gathered skirt, V-shaped neckline, white piqué collar matching cuffs on short dolman sleeves, tailored belt with self-fabric buckle. Flesh-coloured nylon stockings. White leather shoes, high heels. **4** Grey cotton gabardine dress, fitted bodice, three-button fastening from waist to under pink and grey checked cotton collar and revers which match cuffs of three-quarter-length dolman sleeves, tailored belt with round buckle, hip-level shaped patch pockets and inverted box pleat in centre front of mid-calf-length flared skirt. Black leather shoes, ankle straps, round toes, high heels. **5** Black and white checked wool dress, fitted bodice, turned-down wing collar, wrist-length dolman sleeves, red leather belt, narrow mid-calf-length skirt, shaped yoke seam with concealed pockets, tiny red silk posy on one shoulder. Black fine straw hat, wide brim. Black leather gloves, handbag and shoes.

Wedding Wear

1 Oyster satin dress, fitted bodice, draped oyster chiffon cummerbund, low V-shaped neckline and shoulders incrusted with pearl and crystal beads, framed with deep bias-cut satin collar, long tight inset sleeves fastened on wrist with row of loops and tiny pearl buttons, flared gored skirt with long back train. Small headdress trimmed with pearl and crystal beads, waist-length and ground-length silk-tulle veils. **2** Cream wild-silk strapless dress, ruched over bust, tight fitted panelled boned bodice and wide flared skirt cut in one piece without waist seam; short bolero, shallow grown-on collar and rounded edges bound with self-fabric, long tight dolman sleeves, point over hand, pearl button fastening. Headdress of wax flowers, waist-length double silk-tulle veil. **3** White silk-chiffon dress, draped boned bodice, removable white lace bolero with scalloped edges and long tight sleeves, gathered skirt. Headdress of fresh flowers to match bouquet, long chiffon veil. **4** Pink silk-satin dress with self-colour all-over pattern, fitted bodice, ruching over bust, wing collar, long tight inset sleeves, draped hip yoke split at front forming back train, flared panelled skirt. Fabric tiara trimmed with pearls, waist-length silk-tulle veil. **5** Dark grey wool tailcoat, single-button fastening, flower worn in buttonhole on lapel, breast pocket with handkerchief. Collarless single-breasted pale grey waistcoat. Grey and black striped wool straight-cut trousers, no turn-ups. White shirt, wing collar. Grey striped cravat and pin. Grey top hat. Grey gloves. Black leather lace-up shoes, no toecaps.

Sports and Leisure Wear

1 Holiday wear. Sleeveless yellow and white striped top, fitted bodice, button fastening to under revers and pointed collar, bound cut-away armholes. Bias-cut tailored shorts, side button fastening, large patch pocket on one side, sewn turn-ups, wide black elasticated cotton belt with metal clasp fastening. Yellow and white fabric headband. Yellow and white striped towelling strap sandals, sling-backs, cork soles. **2** Country wear. Dark green and brown tweed double-breasted sports jacket, three-button fastening, inset sleeves, button trim, three angled flap pockets, breast pocket. Straight-cut trousers, no turn-ups. Cream cotton collar-attached shirt. Striped wool tie. Beige felt cap with small peak. Leather lace-up shoes, no toecaps. **3** Holiday wear. Pale blue and cream checked sleeveless dress, slightly bloused bodice, curved yoke seam edged with plain white cotton to match collar and bow tie, covered buttons, tailored belt, covered buckle and edges of large hip-level pocket flaps, gathered mid-calf-length skirt, bias-cut side panels, bias-cut shoulder yoke. White cotton headband. Pale blue canvas shoes, peep toes, ruched decoration, sling-backs, high heels. **4** Beach wear. Hand-knitted pale green cotton sleeveless waist-length top, wide off-the-shoulder collar with fringed edge. Mid-calf-length fitted green linen trousers with turn-ups, hip-level welt pockets. Orange silk headscarf. Cream canvas shoes, rope soles. **5** Golf. Green wool blouse, small collar and buttoned strap opening edged with braid to match hems of dolman sleeves. Straight-cut tan wool trousers, deep waistband, rust leather belt, hip-level welt pockets, turn-ups. Brown leather shoes, buttoned strap, flat heels.

Underwear and Negligee

1 Pale pink cotton brassiere, seamed and darted cups, elasticated side panels, back fastening, adjustable shoulder straps. Pale pink cotton corselette, high waist, light boning, elasticated control panels, side hook fastening, adjustable suspenders. Flesh-coloured nylon stockings. Satin house shoes. **2** Two-piece green and white spotted silk pyjama suit: sleeveless top, wide yoke edged with plain white frill trimmed with fine lace to match hem of gathered top, bound neckline and rouleau bow tie fastening match yoke edge and fastening; trousers gathered from wide waistband into buttoned cuffs on ankles, side hip fastening. Flat satin pumps. **3** Pale peach silk nightdress patterned with self-coloured sprays of flowers, bodice ruched and smocked from waistline to under bust, bra-style top edged with lace, wide shoulder straps, bow trim, full-length gathered skirt, hem decorated with gathered frill edged with lace. Satin ballet pumps. **4** White cotton brassiere, stitched and wired cups, elasticated side panels, back fastening, adjustable shoulder straps. Mid-calf-length pleated white nylon waist-slip, deep waistband with light boning, side fastening. Shoes with round toes, high heels. **5** Two-piece blue and red striped cotton pyjama suit: hip-length single-breasted shirt-style jacket, pearl four-button fastening, small lapels, pointed collar, wide shoulder yoke, long inset sleeves, sewn cuffs, three shaped patch pockets, self-fabric tie-belt; long shorts with stitched cuffs. Red and black leather step-in house slippers.

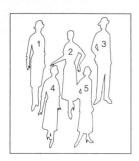

1953 Day Wear

1 Grey flannel dress, fitted bodice, neckline scooped to below bustline, infilled with white piqué blouse, button fastening, large pointed collar, cuffs show under three-quarter-length cuffed dolman sleeves of dress, narrow fitted skirt, diagonal hip-level welt pockets, wide grey suede belt with self-fabric buckle. Brimless draped white silk hat. Grey suede gloves. Black leather shoes with round toes. **2** Pale blue linen dress, slightly bloused panelled bodice, short dolman sleeves, bust-level step opening, three self-fabric buttons, shirt collar, mid-calf-length knife-pleated skirt from fitted hip yoke, wide navy-blue leather belt, metal buckle. Navy-blue leather shoes, round toes, high heels. **3** Dark grey wool three-piece suit: double-breasted jacket, narrow lapels, small collar, fitted sleeves, three-button trim; collarless single-breasted waistcoat, welt pockets, pointed hem; straight-cut trousers, no turn-ups. Collar-attached shirt. Plain silk tie. Dark blue trilby, black band. Black leather lace-up shoes, toecaps. **4** Collarless cream silk dress, elbow-length semi-inset sleeves, fitted bodice, centre-front concealed opening between buttoned notches at neck and waistline, mid-calf-length flared skirt, side panel seams form hip-level pockets. Brown leather shoes, scalloped front detail, round toes, high heels. **5** Two-piece red wool suit: unfitted single-breasted hip-length jacket, five-button fastening to under shirt collar, side panel seams end at diagonal welt pockets, wide inset sleeves, drop shoulderline, narrow cuffs; mid-calf-length flared gored skirt. Small brimless black felt hat. Black silk neckscarf. Black leather shoes.

Evening Wear

1 Mid-calf-length black lace cocktail dress, black silk-taffeta strapless underbodice and flared underskirt, fitted lace bodice, high round neckline trimmed with black velvet ribbon band to match bow tie and narrow belt, drop shoulderline forms short cap sleeves, flared skirt follows line of underskirt worn over stiffened petticoats. Black velvet shoes, shaped fronts above round toes, high heels. **2** Black corded-silk cocktail dress, sleeveless oyster satin bodice, wrapover forms low V-shaped neckline, pleated cummerbund to under bust, fitted mid-calf-length skirt. Elbow-length black silk gloves. Black satin shoes, round toes, high heels. **3** Pale pink satin ball gown, panelled bodice and full-length flared skirt cut in one piece without waist seam, wide off-the-shoulder V-shaped neckline framed with large stole collar, trimmed at centre front with self-fabric bow and posy of silk violets. Above-elbow-length pink suede gloves. Matching costume jewelry set: pearl clip-on earrings, necklace, bracelet. **4** Full-length black velvet evening dress, sleeveless fitted bodice, wrapover effect to one side, self-fabric bow trim, low scooped neckline, straight skirt gathered from low curved waist seam, unpressed knife pleat from side front. Above-elbow-length black silk gloves. Clip-on earrings. Bead necklace. Black satin strap sandals. **5** Red silk cocktail dress, slightly bloused bodice, wide off-the-shoulder neckline forming short sleeves, gathers over bust, black velvet ribbon belt and bow, mid-calf-length gathered skirt from fitted hip yoke worn over stiffened petticoats. Gold hoop earrings. Gold and black bracelet. Black satin shoes, round toes, high heels.

Sports and Leisure Wear

1 Country wear. Long wrapover light brown sheepskin jacket, cream wool shawl collar matching cuffs of long inset sleeves, wide self-fabric belt, leather covered buckle, side panel seams, hip-level diagonal welt pockets, top-stitched edges and detail. Brown knitted-wool sweater. Mid-calf-length brown and yellow checked wool skirt. Brimless beige knitted-wool hat, wired edge, trimmed at back with self-fabric tassel. Brown leather shoes, strap-and-buckle fastening, flat heels. **2** Golf. Dark brown wool shirt, large box-pleat patch pockets with buttoned flaps, sleeves worn rolled to elbow, shoulder yoke, pointed collar worn open, top-stitched detail. Plain cream silk cravat. Straight-cut beige cavalry-twill trousers, side hip pockets, turn-ups, brown leather belt. Brown leather shoes. **3** Holiday wear. Red denim pinafore dress, wide shoulder straps decorated with blue ricrac braid to match edges of neck and outsized patch-and-buttoned flap pockets, gathered skirt, wide red suede belt. White and red spotted cotton blouse, stand collar, strap opening, cap sleeves. Red leather sandals. **4** Holiday wear. White cotton blouse, shirt collar worn open, three-quarter-length sleeves gathered into buttoned cuffs. Short sleeveless blue cotton bolero decorated with appliqué motifs. Mid-calf-length striped fitted tight trousers, hip-level pockets in side panel, wide waistband. Large blue straw hat, red ribbon trim. Red leather mules. **5** Golf. Black and cinnamon checked brushed-wool hip-length jacket, double-breasted front panel, large collar, inset sleeves, stitched cuffs, decorative top-stitching. Dark grey jersey-wool tight trousers, wide turn-ups. Leather shoes, strap-and-buckle fastening, flat heels.

Accessories

1 Silver kid evening shoes, ankle straps, peep toes, perforated decoration, high heels. **2** Pale blue leather sling-back shoes, peep toes, perforated decoration. **3** Tan leather shoes, strap-and-button trim. **4** Brown suede shoes, leather trim, high heels. **5** Leather sling-back shoes, peep toes, flat heels. **6** Leather shoes, bar strap and buckle, perforated decoration. **8** Navy-blue leather shoes, self-bow trim, top-stitched detail. **7** Black leather shoes, top-stitched detail, high heels. **9** Cream leather shoes, top-stitched strap, navy-blue platform soles and low wedge heels. **10** Leather handbag, double leather handles, clasp fastening. **11** Cream leather handbag, tan suede top and handle. **12** Red leather shoes, ruched fronts, button trim, peep toes. **13** Leather handbag, double rouleau handles, clasp fastening. **14** Black grosgrain evening bag, rouleau handles, clasp fastening. **15** Brimless straw hat trimmed with velvet leaves and plastic berries. **16** Cream felt hat, curled brim, red petersham ribbon trim. **17** Two-tone felt hat, small red crown, white silk trim, wide white brim, red rose trim. **18** Brown leather shoes, strap-and-buckle fastening, top-stitched detail. **19** Brown leather golf shoes, strap-and-buckle fastening, fringed tongues, perforated decoration. **20** Brimless yellow straw hat, white pom-pon trim. **21** Brushed-felt hat, brown brim, self-fabric rouleau band and bow. **22** Black suede ankle-boots, lined and trimmed with fur, high heels. **23** Leather brogues, perforated decoration. **24** Leather shoes, top-stitched detail, toecaps. **25** Embroidered cloth shoes, open sides, peep toes, flat heels. **26** Elastic-sided black suede ankle-boots, lined and trimmed with fur, leather soles, high heels.

1954 Day Wear

1 Three-piece striped blue cloth suit: single-breasted jacket, three-button fastening, narrow lapels; collarless single-breasted waistcoat, welt pockets; straight-cut trousers, narrow hems, turn-ups. Red and white striped collar-attached shirt. Blue silk tie. Black trilby. Black shoes. **2** Wrapover black cotton piqué dress, fitted bodice, wide V-shaped neckline, cap sleeves, shiny black and white buttons, mid-calf-length straight skirt, black patent-leather belt. Small black straw hat, white trim. Elbow-length black cotton gloves. Black leather shoes, peep toes, patent-leather trim, high heels. **3** Red wool button-through dress, fitted bodice to under bust, dolman top with stand collar and elbow-length sleeves, red leather covered buttons from collar to above hemline, flared skirt with panels of knife pleats. Cream straw hat, wide bonnet brim, tall crown draped with red silk. Red leather shoes, round toes, high heels. **4** Royal-blue and black wool-tweed two-piece suit: single-breasted jacket, shiny black buttons from waistline to under narrow collar, fitted bodice, concealed pockets set into seams on side hip below waistline, mock buttoned flap pockets below rounded shoulderline, dolman sleeves, deep cuffs; straight skirt. Royal-blue felt beret with stalk. Black cotton gloves. Black leather sling-back shoes, round toes, high heels. **5** Navy-blue showerproof cotton raincoat, red and silver buttons from waistline to under rounded revers, peter-pan collar worn turned up, inset sleeves, deep cuffs, large patch pockets with mock flaps, red saddle-stitched edges and detail. Red and white patterned silk scarf. Small navy-blue felt hat, low crown, red petersham trim. Navy-blue leather gloves and shoes.

Evening Wear

1 Full-length unfitted red velvet evening coat, boat-shaped neckline and hip-length armholes edged with wide band of embroidered and beaded decoration, three-button fastening below neckline, unpressed box pleats from neck to hem, short back train. Long black kid leather gloves. Costume jewelry: clip-on drop earrings, matching bracelet. **2** Two-piece black wool evening suit: waisted double-breasted jacket, silk lapels matching covered buttons, piped pockets; straight-cut trousers, narrow hems, no turn-ups. White collar-attached shirt. Narrow black silk bow-tie. Black patent-leather shoes. **3** Black cotton gabardine evening dress, strapless boned bodice, neckline edged with white grosgrain flap matching band and large bow at above knee-level on full panelled skirt which is worn over stiffened petticoats. Long black kid leather gloves. Bead necklace. Clip-on earrings. **4** Silver and white cotton-piqué evening dress, hip-length fitted boned bodice, low scooped neckline to below bust infilled with ruched self-fabric, wide shoulder straps cut in one piece with side panels of bodice, full-length narrow skirt, draped over hips, unpressed flared box pleat at back. Matching set of costume jewelry: clip-on earrings, necklace, bracelet. White kid gloves. Shoes with peep toes. **5** Mid-calf-length pink taffeta cocktail dress, fitted boned bodice to under bust, unpressed self-fabric frill standing up over bust, wide skirt cut in flared panels forming V-shape on hipline, self-fabric button trim on side hips. Drop earrings. Long navy-blue silk gloves. Navy-blue satin sling-back strap sandals.

Sports and Leisure Wear

1 Beach wear. One-piece multicolour-spotted white stretch-cotton bathing costume, strapless boned fitted top, stitched and wired cups, panel seams, short gathered drawers from piped V-shaped hip seam. Towelling mules, peep toes, rope soles. **2** Ski wear. Wind and rainproof yellow ribbed cotton-poplin top, elasticated waistline, wide stand collar, inset sleeves with drop shoulderline, single piped pocket at bust-level with zip fastening to match pockets in skirt. Narrow black jersey trousers, stitched creases. Brimless black knitted-wool hat, wide turned-back rib. Hand-knitted black and yellow wool mittens. Fur-lined and trimmed ski-boots. **3** Tennis. Hand-knitted white cotton sweater, V-shaped neckline, cuffed raglan sleeves. White cotton collar-attached shirt, pointed collar worn open. Tailored white cotton-poplin shorts, diagonal side pockets, no turn-ups. Knitted white ankle socks. White canvas lace-up sports shoes, rubber soles. **4** Holiday wear. White glazed-cotton sundress printed with multicoloured roses, fitted bodice, halter neckline gathered into one-piece fitted cup, mid-calf-length flared panelled skirt, self-fabric tailored belt and self-fabric buckle. Triangular cape in matching fabric edged with black cotton fringe. Flat leather pumps, bow trim. **5** Golf. Hip-length brushed-wool jacket, zip fastening from hem to under large peter-pan collar worn turned up, cuffed raglan sleeves, asymmetric patch pockets, buttoned welt, top-stitched edges and detail. Ankle-length light-brown jersey fitted tight trousers. Light brown wool hat, narrow ribbed brim. Brown leather shoes, fringed tongues, flat heels.

Underwear and Negligee

1 Knee-length gold silk dressing gown patterned with black and brown motifs, wrapover front, shawl collar, three patch pockets, cuffed inset sleeves, self-fabric tie-belt. Black and gold silk pyjamas. Black velvet step-in slippers, satin binding. **2** Cream silk pyjama suit: hip-length single-breasted jacket, shoulder yoke, pink satin pointed peter-pan collar which matches strap fastening, welts of shaped breast-level patch pockets and hems of inset sleeves; wide ankle-length trousers. Pink fake-fur mules, cross-over fronts, peep toes. **3** Pale yellow crêpe-de-chine waist-length camisole patterned with sprigs of cream flowers, V-shaped neckline edged with cream lace to match hemline, satin ribbon shoulder straps and bow trim, side fastening. Half-slip in matching fabric gathered from elasticated waistband, lace-edged hem, satin ribbon bow trim. Cream velvet and satin mules, peep toes, high heels. **4** Full-length pale blue cotton-voile nightdress patterned with pink and cream flower sprays, deep cream lace yoke, plain cream cotton-satin peter-pan collar which matches rouleau pipings and bindings, bow tie of keyhole opening and tie-belt, bloused bodice, gathered skirt. Cream satin pumps, bow trim. **5** Waist-length fine white cotton camisole patterned with pale pink, fitted bra top, narrow shoulder straps, side fastening. Knickers in matching fabric, ruched and elasticated waistband, flared legs edged with pleated frill. Pink satin mules, pink feather trim, high heels.

1955 Day Wear

1 Collarless off-white silk-tweed dress, long fitted bodice, short cap sleeves, two mock flap pockets set into hip seam, fitted tapered skirt. Brimless red felt hat trimmed with silk leaves and berries. Large clip-on earrings. Brooch worn below shoulderline. Elbow-length red suede gloves. Long wild mink stole. Red suede shoes, round toes, high heels.
2 Two-piece red wool suit: long fitted double-breasted jacket fastening with metal buttons from hip-level to under black fur collar, matching fur muff worn on one sleeve, hip-level vertical welt pockets; narrow skirt. Brimless black velvet hat. Long umbrella. Black leather shoes. 3 Knee-length single-breasted raincoat, vertical welt pockets in upper body, patch-and-flap pockets in skirts, inset sleeves, half straps, button trim, self-fabric buckled belt, multi-lines of top-stitching on hem, top-stitched edges and detail. Narrow trousers, no turn-ups. Step-in shoes. 4 Charcoal-grey flannel two-piece suit: hip-length unfitted jacket, single-breasted fastening from hipband to under stiff white cotton collar, large grey and white striped silk bow, three-quarter-length sleeves cut in one piece with panelled bodice, half strap, button trim; sunray-pleated skirt. Brimless black felt hat. Short white cotton gloves. Black leather shoes.
5 Two-piece green linen suit: edge-to-edge flared jacket, wide lapels buttoned over large square collar, three-quarter-length cuffed sleeves, button trim, vertical welt pockets; fitted dress, wrapover buttoned collar, fitted tapered skirt. Brimless black felt hat, brooch trim. Black fabric gloves. Black leather shoes, peep toes, high heels.

Evening Wear

1 Brick-red silk-taffeta strapless ball gown, asymmetric draped shoulder cape, long fitted boned bodice, draped hip yoke forming long sash to one side, full-length skirt gathered from hipline worn over stiffened petticoats. Long black silk gloves. 2 White embossed-silk evening dress, wide shoulder straps, straight neckline with wide V-shaped cut in centre front, fitted bodice, seam under bust, no waist seam, flared skirt with large pale pink satin bow between each side panel seam at knee-level. Costume jewelry: large drop earrings, black and white stones set in silver; matching necklace. Long black silk gloves. White satin shoes. 3 Gold lurex brocade blouse, off-the-shoulder neckline framed with deep collar and large knotted tie, fitted hip-level bodice with panel seams, open seams at hip-level, tight elbow-length sleeves. Floor-length black duchess-satin wide flared skirt. Black satin shoes. 4 Pale sky-blue duchess-satin cocktail dress, fitted boned bodice, shaped seam under bust, narrow rouleau shoulder straps end in tiny self-fabric bows, mid-calf-length flared skirt, wide front panel with two hip-level concealed pockets. Long cream satin gloves. Pale sky-blue satin shoes, round toes trimmed with self-fabric rosebuds, high heels. 5 Cream silk cocktail dress, hip-length fitted bodice embroidered with rows of rhinestones to match undercollar and short sleeves, off-the-shoulder neckline edged with narrow collar which matches hip-level cuff above gathered mid-calf-length skirt worn over stiffened petticoats. Pearl stud earrings with matching bracelets. Cream satin shoes, round toes, high heels.

Sports and Leisure Wear

1 Football. Black, orange, grey and white horizontally striped machine-knitted shirt, long inset sleeves, ribbed cuffs, white cotton collar with three-button strap opening. Baggy white cotton shorts, fly opening, side hip pockets. Striped knitted-wool socks matching colours in shirt. Brown leather ankle-boots, hard toecaps, pegged soles. 2 Beach wear. Patterned elasticated-cotton bathing costume, hip-length fitted bodice, plain white elasticated-cotton halter straps which fasten at back and match narrow cuff on straight neckline and band at hip-level above short flared skirt. Brimless green raffia hat with pointed crown. Clip-on plastic flower-shaped earrings. Green canvas sling-back shoes, white trim, flat heels. 3 Holiday wear. White glazed-cotton dress patterned with sprays of lilac flowers, fitted collarless bodice and full flared skirt cut in one piece, V-shaped neckline forms mock wrapover bodice and button fastening ending in deep unpressed box pleat in centre front of skirt, short cap sleeves. Lilac straw hat, shallow crown, wide brim. White plastic hoop earrings. Short transparent white nylon gloves. White canvas shoes, open lapel-effect fronts, lilac button trim. 4 Tennis. White cotton blouse, self-fabric buttons, rounded grown-on collar, short cap sleeves. Short flared white cotton-poplin skirt, grown-on waistband, threaded buckle fastening, side hip pockets incorporated into short curved side panel seams, top-stitched detail. White cotton ankle socks. White canvas sports shoes. 5 Country wear. Hip-level hand-knitted brick-red wool sweater, outsized cowl collar, drop head inset sleeves, ribbed hems. Knee-length black wool tight knee breeches with turn-ups. Knee socks, diamond-shaped pattern. Black leather pumps, bow trim, flat heels.

Accessories

1 Green ribbed knitted-wool ski-hood. 2 Brown leather ankle-boots, dark brown knitted-wool scalloped yokes, thick soles, small heels. 3 Brimless hat draped in black silk, flat top, brooch trim. 4 Bright pink silk rose worn as evening hat. 5 Hand-knitted royal-blue wool peaked ski-cap, deep cuff side and back, pom-pon trim. 6 Grey leather handbag, side-to-side zip fastening over top, strap-and-brass clasp over fastening at centre. 7 Black velvet hat, pointed crown, fur brim. 8 Crownless navy-blue rough straw hat. 9 Gold brocade evening mules, high wedge heels. 10 Brown leather shoulder bag, flap-and-clip fastening, long handle. 11 Grey leather shoes, asymmetric half straps, central seam, top-stitching. 12 Red leather shoes, narrow self-strap, perforated decoration, low heels. 13 Tan suede shoes, tan leather piping, medium heels. 14 Cream leather shoes, top-stitched detail, brown leather button trim, flat heels. 15 Small pink felt hat, narrow upturned brim. 16 Short pink cloth gloves, satin ribbon and bow trim. 17 Yellow canvas shoes, self-fabric central strap with black fringe, black button trim, flat heels. 18 Navy-blue lace evening shoes, satin trim, peep toes. 19 Black suede shoes, hand top-stitching, low sides, high heels. 20 Short red leather gloves, cuffs trimmed with tiny black buttons and braid. 21 Brimless hand-knitted cream wool hat, flat top, tassel trim. 22 Small grey silk evening hat, draped crown, wired velvet leaves on each side. 23 Brown leather shoes, crossed strap fronts, open sides, perforated decoration, high heels. 24 Light brown sling-back half-sandals, shaped fronts, peep toes, medium heels. 25 White canvas shoes spotted in green, low sides, button trim, flat heels. 26 Large brown leather handbag, shaped sides, top-stitching, single strap, clip fastening.

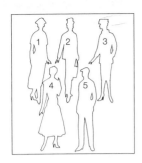
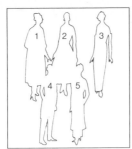

1956 Day Wear

1 Two-piece lilac linen suit: hip-length double-breasted jacket, button fastening from waistline to under bust, rounded grown-on collar and upper shoulder panel of short dolman sleeves cut in one piece, sewn half cuffs and narrow front panel to bust-level, fitted bodice and jacket skirt cut without waist seam, cut-away front; narrow skirt. Deep lilac straw hat, sloping brim, tiny crown. Purple suede gloves. Matching purple suede outsized handbag with double handles. Matching purple suede shoes with high heels. **2** Two-piece cream wool suit: unfitted single-breasted collarless jacket, fastening with four outsized buttons, long raglan sleeves, side hip-level self-fabric trim; narrow skirt. Large cream leather handbag, rouleau handle. Matching cream leather shoes, round toes, button trim, high heels. **3** Two-piece green and brown tweed suit: hip-length unfitted jacket, single-breasted fastening to under fur collar, two welt pockets above bustline, inset three-quarter-length two-piece sleeves, button trim, self-fabric tie-belt on low waistline; narrow skirt. Brimless brown velvet hat, self-fabric bow trim on back. Three-quarter-length brown leather gloves. Matching brown leather shoes. **4** Pea-green cotton dress, low neckline, black glazed-cotton scarf tied under large self-fabric collar, elbow-length inset sleeves, bodice fitted from hipline to under bust, gathered top, full skirt. Black leather shoes, shaped fronts, high heels. **5** Tan wool-tweed single-breasted sports jacket, two-button fastening, flap pockets, breast pocket. Light brown cavalry-twill straight-cut trousers with turn-ups. Collar-attached cream cotton shirt. Green wool tie. Brown wool fitted cap, small peak. Light brown suede lace-up shoes.

Evening Wear

1 Wrapover red velvet evening coat, flared from shoulder to wide mid-calf-length hem, shawl collar, inset three-quarter-length sleeves gathered into deep fitted cuffs, hip-level bound pockets. Small hat, beaded red silk pointed crown, padded roll brim matching coat fabric. Costume jewelry: clip-on bead earrings, matching necklace. Black satin gloves. Black satin shoes. **2** Black satin cocktail dress, low wide neckline, tight three-quarter-length inset sleeves, upper bodice ruched and gathered to central self-fabric bar forming bow-effect, fitted lower bodice and bell-shaped skirt cut in flared panels without waist seam. Large bead earrings, matching pendant necklace. Black satin shoes, peep toes. **3** Black crêpe evening dress, fitted bodice, wide shoulder straps, narrow flat rouleau self-fabric belt, bow tie on centre front of waist, straight ankle-length panelled skirt gathered on side waist. Long black silk gloves. Matching black silk shoes, pointed toes. **4** Edge-to-edge black wool tailcoat, two linked-button fastenings, silk lapels. Collarless single-breasted white piqué waistcoat. Straight-cut trousers, black satin ribbon stripe on outside seam, no turn-ups. Collar-attached white cotton shirt, large bow-tie matching handkerchief in breast pocket. Black patent-leather lace-up shoes. **5** Strapless cream silk evening gown, high waist marked with self-fabric flat rouleau bow, mid-calf-length flared overskirt, split on centre front, straight ankle-length underskirt. Costume jewelry: large earrings, necklace. Long cream silk gloves. Cream satin shoes, pointed toes.

Sports and Leisure Wear

1 Golf. Hip-length beige machine-knitted wool collarless jacket, zip fastening from wide ribbed welt to under V-shaped neckline, bloused body with brown washable-suede side panels from shoulders to sloping welt pockets, cuffed inset sleeves. Beige cavalry-twill straight-cut trousers, narrow hems, no turn-ups. Collar-attached cream brushed-cotton shirt. Brown wool tie. Light brown wool-tweed peaked cap. Brown leather lace-up shoes. **2** Golf. Hip-length dark green suede sleeveless jerkin top, V-shaped neckline, hip-level self-fabric tie-belt, large hip-level patch-and-flap pockets. Collarless machine-knitted beige wool sweater, long cuffed inset sleeves. Brown wool trousers, narrow hems. Brown leather shoes, flat heels. **3** Beach wear. Multicoloured diamond-patterned glazed cotton blouse, low wide neckline, mock-button fastening on bustline, short kimono sleeves. Knee-length trousers in matching fabric, wide waistband, side fastening. **4** Country wear. Light brown machine-knitted wool cardigan-jacket, wide button fastening from wide ribbed welt to under V-shaped neckline, small ribbed collar matching cuffs of long inset sleeves. Cream and beige checked silk neckscarf. Green, beige and brown checked wool-tweed flared panelled skirt. Beige wool stockings. Brown leather lace-up shoes. **5** Holiday wear. Yellow cotton-poplin dress, low sweetheart neckline, ruched bra-top which matches shoulder straps with frilled edges, white piping and rouleau bow trim, hip-length fitted pintucked bodice trimmed with white buttons, full gathered yellow poplin skirt patterned with garlands of green and white flowers. Yellow canvas mules, platform soles, low wedge heels.

Underwear and Negligee

1 Full-length red brushed-cotton dressing gown, wide curved cross-over yoke edged with red nylon pleating to match trim on cuffs of three-quarter-length sleeves and tops of large hip-level patch pockets, two-button diagonal fastening on yoke edge, self-fabric belt fastening in large bow on side waist, flared skirt. **2** White nylon brassiere, stitched undercups, elasticated panels side and back, lace trim, adjustable shoulder straps, back fastening. White nylon girdle, front control panel, elasticated waistband and side panels, four adjustable suspenders, lace trim. Flesh-coloured nylon stockings. Shoes with peep toes, medium heels. **3** White nylon slip, hip-length fitted bodice, narrow ribbon shoulder straps, lace trim which matches hem of three-tier gathered skirt. Satin shoes, medium stiletto heels. **4** Two-piece green and white cotton pyjama suit: unfitted jacket gathered from rounded off-the-shoulder yoke seam, single-breasted three-button fastening to under shawl collar, three-quarter-length full inset sleeves gathered into contrasting colour cuffs which match yoke and flaps of hip-level patch pockets; green knee-length trousers, contrasting colour hems. Green velvet house slippers, flat heels. **5** Pale blue nylon sleeveless nightdress, V-shaped neckline, pleated collar which matches front bodice panel from yoke seam to wide inset waistband and front and back panels of full-length skirt, armholes edged with ruched nylon to match edges of collar and neckline. Satin slippers with cross-over straps and peep toes.

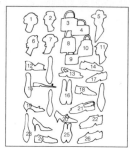

1957 Day Wear

1 Olive-green wool-tweed two-piece suit: knee-length single-breasted unfitted jacket, three large buttons from hip-level to under narrow revers, large collar, long raglan sleeves, hip-level flap pockets; straight skirt. Patterned silk scarf at neck. Brimless orange velvet hat, large crown gathered into wide band. Short brown leather gloves; matching outsized handbag; matching shoes, narrow bar straps, pointed toes. 2 Pale grey lightweight wool dress, button-through fitted bodice, small wing collar, red nylon-chiffon bow tie, three-quarter-length inset sleeves, narrow cuffs, button trim, wide stiffened self-fabric belt, metal buckle, unpressed pleats from waist of bell-shaped skirt, stiffened petticoats. 3 Two-piece cream wool-jersey suit: single-breasted semi-fitted jacket, wide rounded revers, front opening and hem bound in red to match covered buttons, two welt pockets above bustline, piped low waist-level pockets set into curved side panel seams, inset sleeves; straight skirt. Draped red wool-jersey turban. Cream cotton gloves. Red leather envelope purse; matching bar-strap shoes, pointed toes, high stiletto heels. 4 Bright pink wool unfitted double-breasted coat, large buttons from hip-level to under large collar, wide inset sleeves, deep split cuffs, pockets set into side seams at hip-level. Brimless black felt hat, brooch trim. Short black leather gloves; matching bar-strap shoes, pointed toes, stiletto heels. 5 Navy-blue linen dress, large self-fabric collar, white cotton piqué over-collar, three-quarter-length sleeves, buttoned cuffs, fitted bodice, self-fabric wide stiffened belt, straight skirt, unpressed pleats from waist. Brimless navy-blue straw hat, white straw leaf trim. White cotton gloves. Navy-blue leather bar-strap shoes, pointed toes, high stiletto heels.

Evening Wear

1 Short white cotton cocktail dress, fitted hip-length bodice, straight neckline edged with white cotton broderie anglaise embroidered in black to match gathered three-tier bell-shaped skirt worn over stiffened petticoats, black velvet ribbon shoulder straps and bow trim on centre-front neckline. White leather bar-strap shoes, pointed toes, stiletto heels. 2 Full-length fine Irish linen ball gown, pale pink fitted boned strapless bodice, edged with self-fabric pleating, deep pink gathered skirt, wide olive-green pleated belt threaded through large self-fabric buckle. 3 White silk evening dress patterned with life-size pink and red roses and rosebuds with long leafed stalks, sleeveless semi-fitted bodice, straight neckline, full-length straight skirt, centre-back kick pleat, wide plain white silk stiffened belt, large self-fabric bow trim. Long white silk gloves. Matching white silk shoes with pointed toes. 4 Short cocktail dress in synthetic taffeta, multicoloured pattern, wide off-the-shoulder wrapover neckline which stands away over shoulder and at back, fitted bodice, front panel from waist to under bust ruched to match short side hip panels in gathered bell-shaped skirt worn over stiffened petticoats, three-quarter-length inset sleeves. Short satin gloves. Matching satin shoes, pointed toes, stiletto heels. 5 Deep pink duchess-satin ball gown, fitted bodice, large stand-away off-the-shoulder wrapover collar, large black velvet rose trim at centre front, full-length bell-shaped skirt, unpressed pleats at side front and back waist. Long silk gloves.

Sports and Leisure Wear

1 Country wear. Single-breasted green and beige wool-tweed jacket, three-button fastening, narrow lapels, three patch pockets. Light brown wool trousers with turn-ups. Beige brushed-cotton collar-attached shirt. Tan wool tie. Beige wool-tweed peaked cap. Brown leather lace-up shoes, no toecaps. 2 Tennis. White synthetic-linen sleeveless blouse, button fastening from waist to under narrow stand collar, curved side panel seams. Short flared skirt in matching fabric, side panel seams form scalloped hemline, top-stitched detail, narrow waistband, threaded tailored self-fabric buckled belt. White cotton ankle socks. White canvas lace-up sports shoes. 3 Beach wear. Strapless elasticated navy-blue nylon and cotton panelled bathing costume, hip-length fitted boned bodice incorporating briefs, white piping over bustline matches rouleau bow on centre front. Orange straw hat trimmed with self-colour raffia, pointed crown, wide brim. 4 Holiday wear. Red and white horizontally striped cotton dress, sleeveless fitted bodice, shallow bias-cut yoke incorporating square neckline, sunray-pleated skirt, horizontal stripes increasing in width to hemline. Red straw hat, tall crown, flat top, self-straw band and bow trim, wide straight brim. Outsized red raffia bag, painted wooden handle, flap-and-stud fastening. Red plastic and rubber mules, straps between toes. 5 Leisure wear. Hip-length blue, green and white striped knitted-cotton sleeveless tunic-top, off-the-shoulder collar, wide blue leather belt with large buckle. Mid-calf-length dark blue cotton tight trousers. Dark blue leather shoes, pointed toes, bow trim, flat heels.

Accessories

1 Grey velvet beret, full crown gathered into padded rouleau band. 2 Black felt hat, small crown, turned-down brim, white feather trim. 3 Large black leather handbag, double rouleau handles, clasp fastening. 4 Yellow leather handbag, double handles, top-stitched flap matching seams and edges, brass fittings. 5 Dark green brushed-wool trilby, plaited band, feather trim. 6 Brimless beige felt hat, white silk band and bow trim. 7 Brown felt hat, small crown, large two-tier fur brim. 8 Large beige leather handbag, sides and flap trimmed in tan leather to match rouleau handle, brass fittings. 9 Blue leather envelope-shaped handbag, small rouleau handle, brass fittings. 10 Large cream leather handbag, strap-and-buckle fastening, wooden handles. 11 Brown wool-tweed peaked cap. 12 Mules, striped canvas crossed straps, high wedge cork heels. 13 Light brown leather sandals, crêpe soles. 14 Tan leather step-in shoes, self-leather bow and trim. 15 Mules, studded instep strap, raised stud worn between two toes, low wedge cork heels. 16 Red leather lace-up shoes, self-leather laces with tassel trim, square toes. 17 Black leather elastic-sided step-in shoes, seamed fronts. 18 Black leather lace-up shoes, pointed toes. 19 Pale blue pearlized leather shoes, low buckled bar strap, pointed toes, medium stiletto heels. 20 Black leather T-strap shoes, pointed toes, high stiletto heels. 21 Dark brown leather sandals, crêpe soles. 22 Beige suede lace-up shoes, synthetic soles. 23 Red leather shoes, low-cut shaped fronts, pointed toes, high stiletto heels. 24 Blue leather lace-up shoes, flat heels, crêpe soles. 25 Beige pearlized leather shoes, double bar straps, pointed toes. 26 Navy-blue leather step-in shoes, self-leather trim, flat heels.

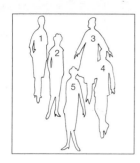

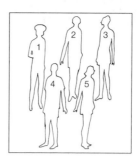
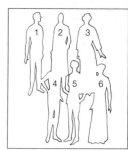

1958 Day Wear

1 Oatmeal silk-tweed two-piece suit: semi-fitted single-breasted jacket fastening with two large buttons, U-shaped neckline with tied roll collar, three-quarter-length magyar sleeves, bust-level mock flap pockets, front panel seams split above hemline; straight skirt to just below knee-level. Draped burnt-orange silk-jersey turban, self-fabric bow trim. Cream suede gloves. Tan leather shoes, buckle trim, pointed toes, medium stiletto heels. **2** Pale blue lightweight wool collarless sack dress, wide self-fabric belt threaded through large buckle under bust, mock strap fastening from hemline to neckline under button trim, short cap sleeves. Cream cotton gloves. Blue pearlized leather T-strap shoes, pointed toes, high stiletto heels. **3** Olive-green, violet and black loosely woven wool-tweed seven-eighths-length single-breasted coat fastening with three outsized buttons from hip-level to under large stand-away collar, wide full-length sleeves with deep armholes, wide self-fabric cross-over buttoned belt from high waist position with fringed ends, hip-level bound pockets. Straight skirt in matching fabric. Olive-green felt beret, wide band. Deep violet leather gloves. Matching deep violet leather bar-strap shoes, pointed toes. **4** Single-breasted grey, black and brown striped wool-tweed jacket, two-button fastening, narrow lapels, flap pockets. Black wool-mixture narrow trousers, no turn-ups. Black knitted-cotton collar-attached shirt. Rust suede tie. Beige suede lace-up ankle-boots. **5** Grey flannel sleeveless sack dress, gathers from under buttoned band at neckline which matches band on narrow hemline, low hip-level mock flap pockets. Black leather shoes, pointed toes, low stiletto heels.

Wedding Wear

1 Ivory silk wedding gown, fitted bodice, self-fabric bow trim on centre front from waist to under bust, low scooped neckline, tight inset sleeves, bell-shaped wrapover overskirt cut away at front to show bell-shaped underskirt, both with unpressed pleats from waist. Ivory velvet bow headdress, waist-length silk-tulle veil. **2** Oyster silk dress, fitted bodice and full-length bell-shaped skirt cut in flared shaped panels without waist seam, high waist marked by wide satin band and bow, shaped seam following line of band over bust, satin-covered buttons from bustline to under high round neckline which match buttons on wrists of tight inset sleeves, points over hands. Headdress of silk flowers and leaves, short veil. **3** White lace wedding gown, fitted bodice, scalloped hems of long tight sleeves match centre front of full-length skirt and edge of low scooped neckline which continues under bust to form bolero effect. Headdress edged with pearls, trimmed with silk flowers, short veil. **4** Short cream satin wedding dress, fitted bodice, off-the-shoulder neckline, draped upperbodice and short sleeves link with self-fabric bows, bell-shaped skirt with unpressed pleats from waist worn over stiffened petticoats. Headdress of silk flowers and loops of ribbon, short veil. Cream satin gloves, bow trim. Matching cream satin shoes, bow trim, pointed toes, low stiletto heels. **5** Short pale pink silk dress, fitted bodice, deep inset waistband, straight neckline, long inset sleeves, bell-shaped skirt with unpressed pleats from waist worn over stiffened petticoats. Headdress of silk flowers, waist-length silk-tulle veil. Satin shoes, pointed toes.

Sports and Leisure Wear

1 Holiday wear. Hip-length unfitted sleeveless cream cotton blouse, low square neckline, narrow hipband, self-fabric bow trim. Fitted navy-blue linen shorts. Cream straw hat, wide turned-up brim bound with navy-blue petersham ribbon. Navy-blue leather mules, wide straps over instep, narrow strap between two toes, flat heels. **2** Tennis. Thigh-length white cotton-mixture sleeveless sack dress, gathers from high yoke seam, pointed collar, bound armholes which match keyhole opening and rouleau bow trim fastening, hip-level flap pockets. White cotton ankle socks. White canvas lace-up sports shoes. **3** Tennis. Thigh-length white linen-mixture dress, hip-length semi-fitted sleeveless bodice, self-fabric button fastening from wide hip-belt to under boat-shaped neckline, shaped panel side seams form knife pleats in flared skirt. White ankle socks. White canvas lace-up sports shoes. **4** Holiday wear. Two-piece pea-green cotton beach suit: single-breasted shirt jacket, button fastening from hip-level to under pointed collar, short inset sleeves, stitched cuffs which match three patch pockets and hems of thigh-length shorts, elasticated waistband, fly opening. Brown leather strap sandals. **5** Tennis. Thigh-length white linen dress, low V-shaped neckline, collar with scalloped edge which matches hem of flared skirt, semi-fitted bodice and skirt cut in flared panels without waist seam, bound armholes. White stretch-fabric headband. White cotton ankle socks. White canvas lace-up sports shoes.

Underwear and Negligee

1 White string-mesh sleeveless singlet, low round neckline, deep scooped armholes. White string-mesh briefs, elasticated waistband, high-cut legs, white knitted-cotton double front panel, side opening. **2** Red, black and yellow checked brushed-cotton travel gown, wrapover front, wide roll collar, full-length cuffed inset sleeves, patch pockets, self-fabric tie-belt. Pale yellow cotton pyjamas. Red leather slippers. **3** Powder-blue brushed-wool full-length housecoat, wrapover front, large single-button fastening under high round neckline, wide three-quarter-length magyar sleeves, hip-level patch pockets, high waistline marked with wide ruched pale blue satin belt and matching covered buckle. **4** White nylon-satin corselette, moulded bra, lace trim matching small control panel under bust, elasticated panels over side hips which match small shaped panels either side of centre front above hem, adjustable shoulder straps, four adjustable suspenders. Flesh-coloured nylon stockings. **5** Pale salmon-pink nylon satin bra, moulded cups, lace trim, adjustable shoulder straps, back fastening. Pale salmon-pink nylon satin lightweight pull-on girdle, deep waistband with curved dip at centre front, elasticated front panel, double top-stitched support, four adjustable suspenders. Flesh-coloured nylon stockings. **6** Pale turquoise nylon nightdress, ruched self-fabric panels under and over bust bound on either side with pale pink nylon to match bow trim and double shoulder straps, curved neckline with lace trim, full-length double layer skirt gathered from high waistline under bust.

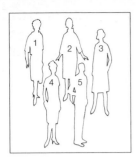

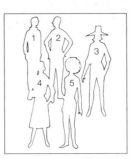

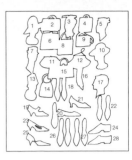

1959 Day Wear

1 Camel-coloured lightweight wool two-piece suit: single-breasted semi-fitted jacket, three outsized buttons, wide neckline, stand-away collar, three-quarter-length magyar sleeves and front panels of jacket cut in one piece, mock flap pockets above side hem; below-knee-level narrow skirt, tucks from waistband. Brimless fur hat. Brown leather gloves. Matching large brown leather handbag, beige trim. Matching brown leather shoes, button trim, pointed toes, high stiletto heels. **2** Brown and black wool-tweed single-breasted coat, fastening with outsized buttons from hip-level to bow trim under high stand collar, three-quarter-length wide dolman sleeves, vertical hip-level welt pockets, hem below knee-level. Brimless burnt-orange felt hat, self-fabric band and button trim. Black gloves. Black patent-leather shoes, ruched bar trim, pointed toes. **3** Two-piece machine-knitted suit patterned with large cream, brown and pale green squares: hip-length sleeveless unfitted top, ribbed V-shaped neckline matching hem; box-pleated skirt. Two-tone brown and cream leather shoes, pointed stitched toecaps. **4** White synthetic-jersey dress patterned with black flowers, high waistline marked with plain white belt threaded through and over with drapery from side hip-level of narrow skirt, low boat-shaped neckline, short inset sleeves. Black brimless pillbox hat. Short white gloves. Black patent-leather Y-strap shoes, pointed toes, high stiletto heels. **5** Two-piece black and grey checked lightweight wool suit: single-breasted jacket, three-button fastening, narrow lapels, flap pockets; straight-cut trousers, narrow hems, no turn-ups. White collar-attached shirt. Blue silk tie and pocket handkerchief. Black leather step-in elastic-sided shoes.

Evening Wear

1 Silk-taffeta short evening dress, all-over design of yellow, cream and ochre stylized roses, fitted and boned strapless bodice joined to bell-shaped skirt by intricate cross-over seaming at waist-level. Long ochre silk stole, fringed hems. Gold kid Y-strap shoes, pointed toes. **2** Pink, silver and smoky-grey patterned brocade theatre coat, edge-to-edge, fastening under self-fabric bow on centre front of wide stand-away collar, coat flared from shoulder to hemline, three-quarter-length flared inset sleeves. Pillbox hat in matching fabric. Long pink suede gloves. Pink silk shoes, pointed toes, high stiletto heels. **3** Single-breasted white linen tuxedo jacket, shawl collar faced with white silk to match single covered button fastening, hip-level piped pockets, inset sleeves, single-button trim. Black linen trousers, narrow hems, no turn-ups, outside seams trimmed with satin ribbon. White collar-attached shirt. Black satin under-collar continental bow-tie. Black lace-up patent-leather shoes, no toecaps. **4** Pale dusty-pink lace short evening dress, fitted overbodice, deep V-shaped neckline, flared sleeves with scalloped hems which match hem of bell-shaped skirt, sleeveless silver-grey satin underdress, low square neckline, bell-shaped skirt to below knee-length worn over stiffened petticoat, wide stiffened-satin cummerbund. Silver kid shoes, pointed toes, medium stiletto heels. **5** Strapless cream duchess-satin ball gown, fitted boned bodice and full-length bell-shaped skirt cut without waist seam, neckline edged with ruched silk-chiffon, beaded and embroidered uneven scalloped seam under bust, repeated on edges of cream velvet inset panel in skirt between hip-level at front and above hemline at back. Long cream silk gloves.

Sports and Leisure Wear

1 Ski wear. Knitted red wool sweater, Fair Isle design in black and white across upper chest and upper arm of inset sleeves, shallow ribbed roll collar which matches sleeve cuffs and hem. Black knitted-wool polo-neck sweater. Black stretch-cloth trousers. Black leather ski-boots. Red wool mittens lined in fur. **2** Ski wear. Pale fawn elasticated cloth all-in-one overall suit, zip fastening from crotch to bust-level under collar and revers, elbow-length cuffed sleeves, top-stitched shoulder dart, decorative buttoned flap, narrow trousers, stitched creases. Bright orange knitted-wool sweater, high round neckline, three-quarter-length sleeves. Balaclava-style hood in bright orange knitted wool. White leather ski-boots. **3** Beach wear. White swiss-cotton two-piece beach suit: shirt blouse, three-quarter-length sleeves gathered into cuffs, bodice printed with three rows of graded brown spots in sets of three on each side of button opening; decoration repeated on fitted shorts, plain white cotton tie-belt. White straw hat, tall crown, wide white cotton band printed with brown spots, wide brim. **4** Holiday wear. Rayon blouse and skirt in bright multicoloured garden print: sleeveless blouse, scooped neckline, drawstring waist; gathered knee-length skirt, plain red tie-belt. Green leather T-strap shoes, pointed toes. **5** Beach wear. Cream linen sunsuit spotted in red, fitted bodice and shorts cut in one piece, side panel seams curve at hip-level to form piped pockets, curved seam over bustline follows shape of neckline, narrow rouleau shoulder straps with matching bow trim. Large natural straw hat, large brim edge trimmed with strands of self-straw.

Accessories

1 Brown brushed-felt hat, large brim, tall crown draped with deep gold chiffon. **2** Brown leather bag, inset leather handles. **3** Brimless grey satin hat, large self-fabric bow trim. **4** Black leather bag, flap with stud fastening, brass trim. **5** Black silk pillbox hat, self-fabric bow trim at back, short black silk-tulle veil. **6** Black leather bag, clasp fastening, long handle. **7** Cherry-red velvet brimless draped hat. **8** Tan leather bag, side zip pocket, top-stitched trim. **9** Green leather and brown canvas shoulder bag, long adjustable strap, strap-and-buckle fastening. **10** Brown felt hat, tall crown, wide fur brim. **11** Gold beaded clutch bag. **12** Brown velvet evening bag gathered into gold beaded frame, gold chain handle. **13** Dark green felt brimless hat, piped trim. **14** Fawn leather unstructured bag, round bamboo handle. **15** Oblong beige hessian bag, brown leather trim which matches rouleau handle, brass fittings. **16** Cream kid gloves, threaded strap trim. **17** Small yellow cloth cap, top-stitched peak. **18** White matt-leather T-strap shoes, perforated decoration, pointed toes. **19** Cream and tan leather bar-strap shoes, pointed toe-caps, high stiletto heels. **20** Navy-blue leather shoes, red binding and bow trim, pointed toes. **21** Dark blue suede shoes, dark blue leather bow trim which matches louis heels. **22** Black leather shoes, fabric asymmetric button trim, pointed toes. **23** Navy-blue leather shoes, open sides, pointed toes, high stiletto heels. **24** Black leather elastic-sided shoes, seamed fronts. **25** Black suede shoes, cut-away sides, pointed toes, high stiletto heels. **26** Sage-green patent-leather shoes, pointed toes, buckled trim. **27** Red patent-leather shoes, key-hole with self-leather bow trim, pointed toecaps. **28** Brown suede step-in elastic-sided shoes, no toecaps.

Chart of the Development of 1950s Fashion

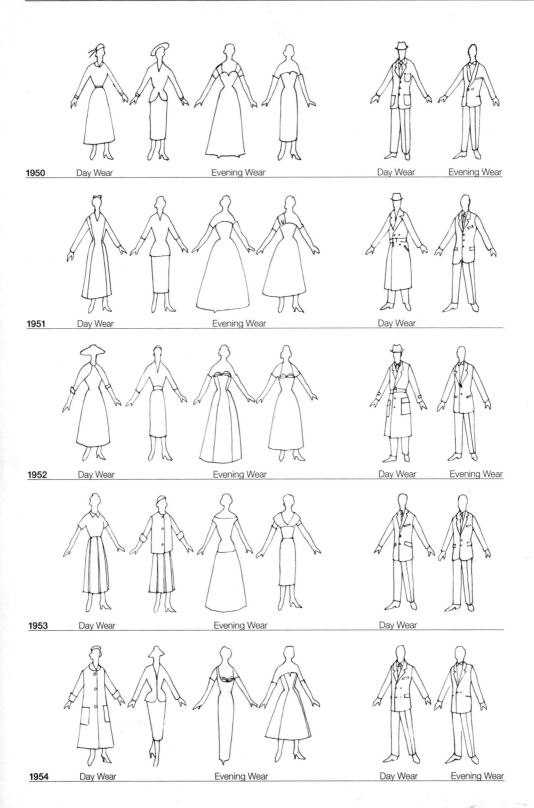

1950   Day Wear   Evening Wear   Day Wear   Evening Wear

1951   Day Wear   Evening Wear   Day Wear

1952   Day Wear   Evening Wear   Day Wear   Evening Wear

1953   Day Wear   Evening Wear   Day Wear

1954   Day Wear   Evening Wear   Day Wear   Evening Wear

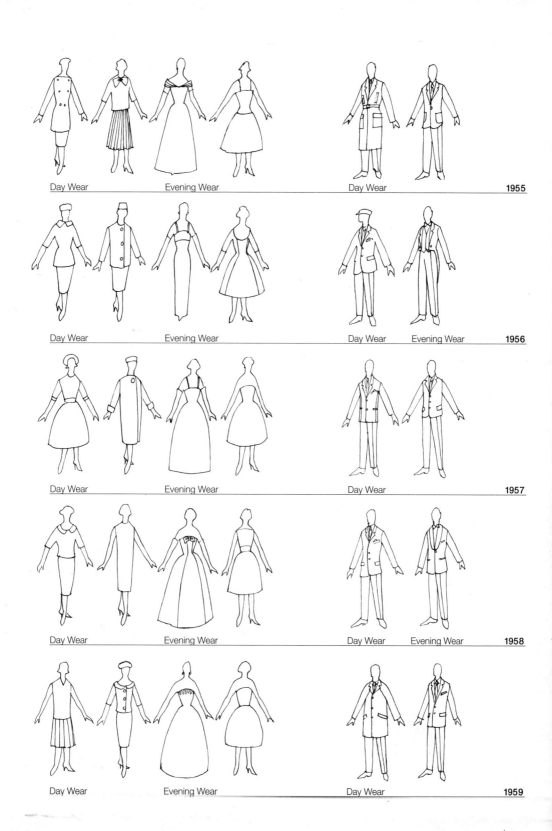

Day Wear   Evening Wear   Day Wear   **1955**

Day Wear   Evening Wear   Day Wear   Evening Wear   **1956**

Day Wear   Evening Wear   Day Wear   **1957**

Day Wear   Evening Wear   Day Wear   Evening Wear   **1958**

Day Wear   Evening Wear   Day Wear   **1959**

Biographies of Designers

Amies, (Sir) Hardy (Erwin)
1909–. Designer. Born London, England. Amies started his career in fashion at Lachasse in 1934. In 1945 he opened his own couture house and became famous for refined, well-cut women's suits in tweed and wool and for sumptuous puff-sleeved ball gowns. He was hugely successful during the 1950s, receiving the Royal Warrant to design clothes for the Queen in 1955. In 1961 he began designing menswear.

Balenciaga, Cristobal
1895–1972. Designer. Born Guetaria, Spain. At the age of 20 Balenciaga opened his first house in San Sebastian. When he moved to Paris in 1936 he was already Spain's leading couturier, producing austere, elegant, well-cut clothes in sombre colours recognizable for their stark Spanish style. In 1939 his tight-waisted dresses with dropped shoulderlines were clear forerunners of Dior's New Look. His main innovations include the pillbox hat, first shown in 1946, the stand-away collar, and the sack dress of 1956. During the 1950s he also began to use lambswool dyed in acid pinks and yellows and made short dresses and coats with dropped hemlines at the back.

Balmain, Pierre (Alexandre)
1914–82. Designer. Born St Jean de Maurienne, France. Balmain started his career with Molyneux. In 1941 he began working at Lelong when he met Dior. When Balmain set up his own couture house in 1945 he created bell-shaped skirts with nipped-in waists similar to those later produced by Dior for the New Look. Though he tended to favour a narrow silhouette for his suits and dresses, Balmain was also known for his full half-belted coats and romantic full-skirted ball gowns. During the 1950s he created his famous sheath dresses, worn under jackets, as well as stoles for day wear and cossack-style wraps.

Cardin, Pierre 1922–. Designer. Born San Biagio Di Callalta, near Venice, Italy, to French parents. Cardin worked for a tailor in Vichy from the age of 17. He moved to Paris in 1944 and found work with Paquin, Schiaparelli and

Dior. In 1947 he designed the costumes for Jean Cocteau's film *La Belle et la bête* and over the following years established a reputation as a theatrical costumier. Cardin opened his own house in 1950 and presented his first collection three years later. During the early 1950s he produced simple elegant couture such as his popular bubble skirts and coats with hemlines dropped at the back. By the 1960s, he had developed into a highly innovative and influential designer for both men and women. In 1964 he showed his avant-garde 'Space Age' collection and became famous for his catsuits, mini-skirts and body stockings.

Cashin, Bonnie 1915–. Designer. Born Oakland, California, USA. Cashin began her career as a costume designer before opening her own business in New York in 1953. She became famous for casual, practical, loose-fitting clothes inspired by her native Californian landscape. Over the next decade she introduced the idea of layered dressing and was acclaimed for mixing natural fabrics such as leather, cashmere, linen and suede. She was also known for her Chinese-style jackets, fringed suede dresses and stylish ponchos.

Cassini, Oleg (Loiewski)
1913–. Designer. Born Paris, France, of Russian parents. Cassini worked in Paris, New York and Hollywood before opening his own firm in 1950. He became famous for glamorous ready-to-wear suits and sheath and cocktail dresses. He was official designer to Jacqueline Kennedy (Onassis) and the two-piece suit with three-quarter-length sleeves that he designed for her was widely copied.

Chanel, Gabrielle (Coco)
1883–1971. Designer. Born in Saumur, France. Chanel began her career as a milliner in Paris in 1910, under the label 'Chanel Mode'. In 1913 she opened her first hat shop in Deauville and two years later started a dress shop in Biarritz. The 1920s saw her career flourish with the founding of her Paris house and the launch of her most famous perfume, 'No. 5'. Chanel was hugely

influential with her 'little black dress', wide-legged yatching pants, geometrically patterned beaded dresses and unconventional mixing of fabrics – plain with patterned jersey, or floral silk with tweed. She also became famous for costume jewelry: her long gilt chains, rows of pearls and mixtures of semi-precious stones were especially popular. Though Chanel closed her house in 1934, when she reopened in 1954 with the launch of her jersey suit, her vision of clothes which combined practicality with elegance was perfectly in tune with the times. During the 1950s she introduced low-heeled, two-tone sling-back pumps and shoulderbags with gilt-chain handles. Her famously wearable tweed suit, which she had created before the Second World War, became a fashion classic and remains so today.

Dessès, Jean (Jean Dimitre Verginie) 1904–70. Designer. Born Alexandria, Egypt, of Greek parents. Dessès began his career at the age of 21 with Maison Jane. He opened his own house in 1937. During the 1950s he was known for his draped evening dresses, inspired by ancient Greek and Egyptian garments, and for his embroidered ball gowns and sheath dresses.

Dior, Christian 1905–57. Designer. Born Granville, France. Dior began his fashion career in Paris at the age of 30, selling fashion sketches to newspapers. He joined Robert Piguet in 1938 and worked briefly for Lelong in 1942 before opening his own house in 1946. In 1947, his first collection, the 'Corolle line', soon nicknamed the 'New Look', was sensationally successful. His curved bodices and huge skirts with nipped-in waists brought a new femininity and glamour to fashion after the severe broad-shouldered, narrow-skirted lines produced under wartime rationing. In the 1950s Dior continued to create highly influential and increasingly sophisticated designs such as three-piece outfits of cardigan, top and skirt, box-shaped jackets with short skirts and his own versions of the caftan and cheongsam. Other widely copied innovations included the

princess line, coolie hats, three-quarter-length sleeves and horseshoe collars.

Fath, Jacques 1912–54. Designer. Born Maison-Lafitte, France. During the 1930s Fath worked as a stockbroker at the Paris Bourse while at the same time studying costume and fashion design. He opened his own house in 1937, achieving worldwide fame by the late 1940s. Fath attracted a young, sophisticated clientele with his extravagant, flirtatious evening dresses and jaunty day clothes, often with decorative pleats, darts and angled collars.

Galanos, James 1924–. Designer. Born Philadelphia, USA. Following a year-long apprenticeship with Piguet in Paris in 1947, Galanos founded his own house, based in Los Angeles, in 1951. His first show in 1953 brought immediate success. He is known for his high standards of tailoring and cutting and for his use of luxurious fabrics. During the 1950s he was innovative in showing suits with horseshoe necklines and evening wear with large prints.

Givenchy, Hubert (James Marcel Taffin) de 1927–. Designer. Born Beauvais, France. After briefly studying law in Paris, Givenchy worked for Fath, Piguet, Lelong and Schiaparelli before opening his own business in 1952. In the 1950s he created many popular designs, including his famous Bettina blouse, his sack dress of 1955 and his sheath dress of 1957. In the course of the decade his young playful style became more sombre under the influence by Balenciaga. Though not among the most innovative of couturiers, Givenchy had a huge influence on womenswear, particularly through his designs for Audrey Hepburn in the 1961 film *Breakfast at Tiffany's*.

Grès, (Madame) Alix
1903–1993. Designer. Born Paris, France. Following her training at Premet, Grès opened her own couture house in 1934 under the name 'Alix', reopening after the Second World War under the name 'Grès'. She became famous for her draped and pleated dresses – in silk and

wool – which resemble classical Greek robes, often cut on the bias and with dolman sleeves. Grès adopted a sculptural approach to dressmaking, each garment being modelled on the mannequin by hand with minimal use of patterns or cutting.

Hartnell, (Sir) Norman
1901–1979. Designer. Born London, England. Hartnell worked at Madame Désirée, Esther's and with Lucile before opening his own premises in London in 1923. He is best known as dressmaker to the British Royal Family and created Elizabeth II's wedding dress and coronation gown as well as many outfits for her overseas tours. He also produced elegantly tailored coats and suits and lavishly embroidered evening gowns.

Heim, Jacques 1899–1967. Designer. Born Paris, France. Heim designed womenswear for his parent's fur business until the 1930s, when he founded his own couture house. He became famous for his 'Atome' two-piece bathing suit of 1950 – the first bikini. He was the first couturier to use cotton for beachwear. During the 1950s he was also known for his halter-neck tops worn with knee-length madras shorts.

James, Charles (William Brega) 1906–78. Designer. Born Sandhurst, England. James began his fashion career when he opened a hat shop in Chicago in 1924 under the name 'Charles Bouchéron'. His created his first dress collection in New York in 1928, his first London collection in 1929, and his first Paris collection in 1934. By 1940 he had returned to New York and established a house under his own name where he based his operation for most of the 1940s and 1950s. An architect of dress, James created superbly cut, sculpted ball gowns using large quantities of lavish fabrics often arranged asymetrically in bunches and folds. He was also well known for his highly structured coats, his dresses with spiral zips and his quilted ivory-satin jackets.

Laroche, Guy 1923–89. Designer. Born La Rochelle, France. Laroche worked in millinery and then for Jean Dessès before opening his own house in 1957. His practical but feminine designs of the late 1950s were highly successful and in 1960 he launched his own ready-to-wear line. He is best known for his fine tailoring and cutting.

Mainbocher (Main Rousseau Bocher) 1891–1976. Designer. Born Chicago, USA. In 1922 Mainbocher was employed by *Harper's Bazaar* as a fashion artist and by 1923 was editor-in-chief of French *Vogue*, a post he held until 1929. Mainbocher was the first American couturier to achieve success in Paris, opening his own salon in 1930. He became famous for embroidered, apron-style evening dresses, for his use of the bias cut and for creating a trend for 'Wallis blue' with the wedding dress he designed for the Duchess of Windsor. Mainbocher opened a salon in New York in 1940. During the 1950s he was best known for his elegant knee-length skirts and for his short jackets with prim bows and peter-pan collars.

Maxwell, Vera (Vera Huppé) 1901–. Designer. Born New York, USA. Maxwell established her business in 1947, creating classic, wearable clothes such as separates and suits, wraparound jersey dresses and riding jackets. She was influenced by men's country clothes and used natural dyes to produce muted, autumnal tones.

McCardell, Claire 1905–58. Designer. Born Frederick, USA. During the late 1920s and 1930s McCardell worked with Richard Turk, at Townley Frocks, and then for Hattie Carnegie. Returning to Townley Frocks in 1940 to design under her own name, McCardell produced easy-fitting clothes made from cotton, denim, gingham and jersey which had a huge impact in the 1950s. Her many popular designs included the 'popover' dress, with side slits and ties; playsuits; dirndl skirts; strapless, elasticated tube tops and the diaper bathing suit. She often used metal fastenings and large patch pockets as decorative details and was the first designer to introduce ballet-type pumps for everyday wear.

Norell, Norman (Norman Levinson) 1900–72. Designer. Born Noblesville, USA. From 1922 Norell worked as a costume designer and for the Seventh Avenue firm Charles Armour. In 1928 he joined Hattie Carnegie, where he remained until he founded Traina-Norell with Anthony Traina in 1941. During the 1940s and 1950s Norell made his reputation as one of America's finest designers, known not only for sophisticated, elaborately trimmed eveningwear but also for his fur trenchcoats, sequined sheath dresses, and empire-line dresses. He founded his own house in 1960.

Pucci, Emilio (Marchese di Barsento) 1914–85. Designer. Born Naples, Italy. In the mid-1940s, as a member of the Italian Olympic ski team, Pucci was photographed by Toni Frissell for *Harper's Bazaar* wearing ski pants he had designed himself. *Harper's Bazaar* then published some of his designs for women's winter clothes which were quickly bought by several New York stores. He founded his own couture house, Emilio, in 1950, producing capri pants, casual suits and other sportswear. Using bold acid colours, Pucci created prints inspired by medieval heraldic banners – psychedelic designs which are now synonymous with the fashions of the late 1950s and 1960s.

Saint Laurent, Yves (Henri Donat Mathieu) 1936–. Designer. Born Oran, Algeria. Saint Laurent's career in fashion took off in 1954 when he won first prize for a design for a cocktail dress in a competition held by the International Wool Secretariat. In 1955 he began working for Dior, taking over the house at the age of 21 when Dior died. Saint Laurent attracted controversy with designs such as his precisely tailored 'Trapeze' dress of 1958 and his leather jackets and turtle-neck sweaters of 1960. Though hugely popular, his youthful style was not appreciated by Dior's more conventional clientele – when he returned from military service in Algeria in 1961 he found he had been replaced by Marc Bohan. Following the establishment of his own house in 1962, Saint Laurent produced a series of innovative

and increasingly sophisticated designs including his influential 'smoking' jacket, see-through blouses, thigh-length boots, velvet knickerbockers, and safari jackets. In 1966 he opened a ready-to-wear chain, Rive Gauche.

Schiaparelli, Elsa 1890–1973. Designer. Born Rome, Italy. Schiaparelli moved to Paris in 1922 and opened a shop, 'Pour le Sport', in 1928. The following year she founded her own couture house, creating chic, eccentric clothes strongly influenced by modern art movements. She commissioned artists such as Salvador Dali and Jean Cocteau to design fabric and accessories and produced a range of surreal garments, often with *trompe-l'œil* effects. Her many innovations included unusually shaped buttons, padlock fastenings, lip-shaped pockets, and hats in the form of icecream cones, shoes or lamb cutlets. In 1933 her broad-shouldered pagoda sleeve set the basic shape for fashion until the New Look. Known for her gifted use of colour, Schiaparelli promoted 'Shocking Pink' and was the first designer to use plastic zippers decoratively. Her last show took place in 1954.

Trigère, Pauline 1912–. Designer. Born Paris, France. Trigère worked for Hattie Carnegie before opening her own house in New York in 1942. Trigère achieved instant success with her finely tailored, original designs. Among her many innovations were removable scarves and collars, dresses with jewelry attached and reversible coats and capes.

Valentina (Valentina Nicholaevna Sanina) 1899–1989. Designer. Born Kiev, Russia. Valentina established her house in 1928. While her daywear was often simple and practical, sometimes displaying peasant influences, she was best known for her dramatic evening wear and swirling capes. She was also a skilled designer of millinery, especially snoods, turbans and veils. During the 1950s Valentina had particular success with her full ballerina-style skirts and slippers.

Sources for 1950s Fashion

Anderson Black, J.
and Madge Garland
A History of Fashion, 1975.

Baynes, Ken,
and Kate Baynes, eds.
The Shoe Show: British Shoes since 1790, 1979.

Boucher, François
A History of Costume in the West, 1965.

Bradfield, Nancy
Historical Costumes of England, 1958.

British Millinery Magazine
British Millinery Exhibition Catalogue, 1957.

Brooke, Iris
A History of English Costume, 1937.

Byrde, Penelope
The Male Image: Men's Fashion in England 1300–1970, 1979.

Carter, Ernestine
The Changing World of Fashion: 1900 to the Present, 1977.

Contini, Mila
Fashion, 1965.

De Courtais, Georgine
Women's Headdress and Hairstyles, 1973.

Dorner, Jane
Fashion in the Forties and Fifties, 1974.

Drake, Nicholas
The Fifties in Vogue, 1987.

Ewing, Elizabeth
History of Twentieth Century Fashion, 1974.
Dress and Undress: A History of Women's Underwear, 1978.
Fur in Dress, 1981.

Fashion Institute of Technology, New York
All American: A Sportswear Tradition, 1985.

Gallery of English Costume
Weddings, 1976.

Ginsburg, Madeleine
Wedding Dress 1740–1970, 1981.
The Hat: Trends and Traditions, 1990.

Hall-Duncan, Nancy
The History of Fashion Photography, 1979.

Howell, Georgina
In Vogue: Six Decades of Fashion, 1975.

Jarvis, Anthea
Brides, Weddings and Customs, 1850–1980, 1983.

Kelsall, Freda
How We Used to Live, 1936–1953, 1981.

Lee-Potter, Charlie
Sportswear in Vogue, 1984.

Lynham, Ruth, ed.
Paris Fashion: Great Designers and Their Creations, 1972.

Mulvagh, Jane
Vogue History of 20th Century Fashion, 1988.

O'Hara, Georgina
The Encyclopaedia of Fashion, 1986.

Peacock, John
Fashion Sketchbook 1920–1960, 1977.
Costume 1066 to the 1990s, 1986.
The Chronicle of Western Costume, 1991.
20th Century Fashion, 1993.
Men's Fashion, 1996.

Robinson, Julian
The Fine Art of Fashion: An Illustrated History, 1989.

Saint Laurent, Cecil
The History of Ladies' Underwear, 1968.

Wilcox, R. Turner
The Dictionary of Costume, 1969.

Yarwood, Doreen
English Costume: From the Second Century to 1967, 1952.

Magazines and Journals
British Millinery, 1956–1958.
Harper's Bazaar (UK), 1950–1959.
Harper's Bazaar (US), 1950–1959.
Idées Détails Couture, 1953–1956.
Officiel de la couleur des textiles de la mode, 1955–1957.
Stella, 1955–1958.
Les Tailleurs et manteaux de Paris, 1951–1954.

Vanity Fair, 1951–1959.
Vogue (France), 1950–1959.
Vogue (UK), 1950–1959.
Vogue (US), 1950–1959.

Haslam, Miss G.A.
The System of Dresscutting, 1950, 1952, 1955, 1958.

Acknowledgments

Thanks are due to Janet Dunham, of Zero Antique Clothes Shop in Newcastle-under-Lyme, for her kindness and help, and for the loan of her many costume magazines.

I also extend my gratitude to the Yale School of Art and Design, Wrexham, Clwyd, for the use of their facilities.